BECOMING A
CONTAGIOUS
CHRISTIAN

PARTICIPANT'S GUIDE

Communicating Your Faith in a Style that Fits You

MARK MITTELBERG, LEE STROBEL & BILL HYBELS
and Wendy Seidman
With contributions by Don Cousins

ZONDERVAN™

GRAND RAPIDS, MICHIGAN 49530

WILLOW
CREEK
RESOURCES

*Helping People Become
Fully Devoted to Christ*

*To the people of Willow Creek Community Church,
whose contagious Christianity inspires us.*

ZONDERVAN™

Becoming a Contagious Christian Participant's Guide
Copyright © 1995 by the Willow Creek Association

Requests for information should be addressed to:

Zondervan, *Grand Rapids, Michigan 49530*

ISBN: 0-310-50101-6

Edited by Rachel Boers

Printed in the United States of America

03 04 05 06 /❖ DC/ 44 43

CONTENTS

Foreword   4

Acknowledgments   5

Session 1   Why Become a Contagious Christian?   7

Session 2   Being Yourself   19

Session 3   Building Relationships   37

Session 4   What's Your Story?   47

Session 5   What's His Story?   59

Session 6   Crossing the Line   71

Session 7   Putting It Together   79

Session 8   Objection!   87

Appendix

Course Evaluation   113

Illustrations   115

Write Out Your Story   122

Keeping the Conversation Going   123

Bibliography   125

FOREWORD

The *Becoming a Contagious Christian* evangelism course is designed to help everyday Christians—like you and me—to confidently and effectively spread their faith to people they know. The emphasis is on natural approaches that work over time to bring family members, friends, co-workers, and neighbors to the point of trusting in Christ.

If you are someone who thinks relational evangelism is very important but "it's not really my area," then we want you to know that this course is *especially* for you. We are convinced that, as you move through these sessions, you will sense a growing excitement about how God can prepare and use *you* to impact the lives of others for eternity.

Through a variety of formats including video vignettes, group discussions, role playing, and teaching segments, you will learn how to communicate the message of Christ in your own personal, God-given style. As you gain confidence and begin to put into action what you have learned, you will discover what thousands of people who have taken this training before you have found out: becoming a contagious Christian is an unparalleled adventure!

You will have the thrill of sensing the Holy Spirit work through you as you build strategic relationships, raise spiritual topics of conversation, express what God has done for you, and encourage your friends toward commitment. When God uses you as part of the team that leads someone across the line of faith, *watch out!* You will never be the same again. You will experience the exhilaration that comes with knowing you have played a key role in fulfilling God's central purpose on earth— "to seek and to save what was lost."

So get ready, roll up your sleeves, and let the adventure begin!

Mark Mittelberg

ACKNOWLEDGMENTS

There are many people at Willow Creek Community Church to whom we owe a debt of gratitude for their encouragement, support, and wide array of contributions to this project.

These include:

- Don Cousins, whose early influence on this project shaped it significantly. Thanks, Don, for the faith, encouragement, and direction.

- Willow Creek's Frontline Evangelism Team, especially the following volunteers: Natalie Allen, Sherry Bohlin, Jack Gallaway, Julie Harney, Charmain Kerrigan, Marie Little, Chad Meister, Michael and Sandy Redding, Julie Schmidt, and Tom and Dee Yaccino. You have helped us in many ways as we've presented this course at the church.

- The Willow Creek drama ministry, especially Donna Lagerquist for her creativity and hard work writing the scripts for the video vignettes, and Steve Pederson for his oversight of the script editing and video recording process.

- Willow Creek staff members Laura Daughtry and Theresa Rozsa, who provided administrative support; and Garry Poole, who added evangelistic insights.

- The Willow Creek elders and board members, who have believed in and tangibly supported the development of this course. In particular, Russ Robinson, for his invaluable advice, feedback, and constructive suggestions.

- Jim Mellado and the Willow Creek Association for facilitating the publishing process and for providing support and encouragement along the way.

- Wendy Guthrie, the Willow Creek Association training expert and the manager of this project, for her tireless efforts in adapting and improving this course for the needs of the wider Christian community.

Also, our deep appreciation to:

- John Nixdorf, of Nixdorf Publishing, for his instructional design skills which he used to make this a more effective training course.

- Lighthouse Productions, for their skillful work at recording and editing the course's video vignettes.

- Zondervan Publishing House, for their partnership in producing and distributing this course for use by churches around the world.

Why Become a Contagious Christian?

OVERVIEW

In Session 1 you will:

1. Describe what Relational Evangelism is not

2. Identify the components of Relational Evangelism

3. Revisit the biblical basis for evangelism

4. Begin an *Impact List* of relationships to build

PERCEPTIONS OF EVANGELISTS

Negative	Positive
pushy combative	Can I do this? Billy Graham People need to Become themselves

RELATIONAL EVANGELISM

1. AUTHENTIC John 15:5

2. _Natural_ Matt 9:9-13

3. _Personal_ LK 9:1-10

4. VERBAL

_And how can they believe in the one of whom they have
not heard? And how can they hear without someone
preaching to them? (Romans 10:14)_ (11-14)

5. _Process-oriented_ John 4:

6. TEAM-ORIENTED   1 Cor. 3:5-9

_A person's coming to Christ is like a chain with many
links. There is the first link, middle links, and a last link.
There are many influences and conversations that
precede a person's decision to convert to Christ. I know
the joy of being the first link at times, a middle link
usually, and occasionally the last link. God has not
called me to only be the last link. He has called me to be
faithful and to love all people._[1]

7. "PUTTING OTHERS FIRST"   - LK 15:3-7

---

[1]Cliff Knechtle (open-air evangelist for InterVarsity Christian Fellowship), _Give Me
An Answer,_ InterVarsity Press, 1986.

VIDEO: WHY BECOME A CONTAGIOUS CHRISTIAN?

1. As you watch the video, listen for the reasons why you would want to become a contagious Christian.

2. Write your responses in the space provided below.

BEGIN AN IMPACT LIST

1. Carefully consider the people in your life to whom you could give concentrated effort in the attempt to bring them to the next step in the evangelism process.

2. List the names of these people in the space below.

_____

_____

_____

_____

_____

_____

_____

_____

_____

Please note that these names will change as these people become Christians or move out of your sphere of influence. This list, therefore, should be an ongoing part of your lifelong evangelism strategy.

Remember it is important to develop *no-strings-attached friendships* with the people on your list. Let them know by word and action that they matter to you, regardless of whether or not they agree with the Christian message.

PRAYING FOR THE PEOPLE ON YOUR IMPACT LIST

Begin to pray for the people on your *Impact List*. Ask God to work in their lives and to give you wisdom on how to effectively reach out to them. In praying for them, keep in mind the following three areas:

Them

Ask God to:

- Pull them toward Himself
- Open their eyes to the emptiness of life without Him
- Help them see their need for forgiveness
- Remove the confusion they have about Him and the life He offers
- Help them grasp the meaning and importance of the cross of Christ
- Open the person's heart to God's love and truth

You

Ask God to:

- Help you live a consistent and attractive Christian life
- Make you authentic and honest as you deal with life's ups and downs
- Give you wisdom in knowing how to approach the relationship
- Expand your knowledge so you will be ready to define and defend the Gospel message
- Grant you appropriate boldness and courage
- Use you to help lead this person into a relationship with Christ

Us

Ask God to:

- Cause depth and trust to grow in the relationship
- Open doors for spiritual conversations
- Guide those conversations in pace, frequency, and content

SESSION SUMMARY

In this session you:

- Described what Relational Evangelism is not

- Identified the components of Relational Evangelism

- Revisited the biblical basis for evangelism

- Began an *Impact List* of relationships to build

SUGGESTED READING: CHAPTERS 1–3

(*Becoming a Contagious Christian* companion book)

For more information on the topics we will cover in each session, we will provide a "Suggested Reading" section from the companion book for this course, *Becoming a Contagious Christian* (by Bill Hybels and Mark Mittelberg, Zondervan, 1994).

For this first session, we encourage you to read the first three chapters. As you'll see, they illustrate and expand upon the principles we're discussing in this course. Other reading suggestions from this book will be listed at the end of later sessions.

Chapter 1 reinforces the value that all people matter to God. Chapter 2 explores the overwhelming rewards of becoming contagious Christians. And Chapter 3 spells out a biblical formula for influencing our worlds for Christ: **HP + CP + CC = MI.** The first element, **HP**, refers to high potency (chapters 4-6 in the book lay out three character traits to help us achieve this). The second is **CP**, which means close proximity with those we hope to influence—we've got to get close to them. The third is **CC**, clear communication of the gospel message itself. As we combine these three things, God will use them to produce **MI**, maximum impact on others.

PREVIEW OF REMAINING SESSIONS

Session 2—Being Yourself

Session 3—Building Relationships

Session 4—What's Your Story?

Session 5—What's His Story?

Session 6—Crossing the Line

Session 7—Putting It Together

Session 8—Objection!

Course Goal: To Become Contagious Christians!
Christians who are equipped with the knowledge and skills needed to effectively communicate our faith.

EVANGELISM STYLES QUESTIONNAIRE

DIRECTIONS

1. Record your response to each of the 36 statements according to whether you think the statement applies to you:

   3 Very much
   2 Somewhat
   1 Very little
   0 Not at all

2. Transfer your responses to the grid at the bottom of page 18 and total each column:

_3_ 1. In conversations, I like to approach topics directly, without much small talk or beating around the bush.

_1_ 2. I have a hard time getting out of bookstores or libraries without getting a bunch of books that will help me better understand issues being debated in society.

_3_ 3. I often tell stories about my personal experiences in order to illustrate a point I am trying to make.

_2_ 4. I am a "people person" who places a high value on friendship.

_3_ 5. I enjoy including or adding new people to activities I am involved in.

_1_ 6. I see needs in people's lives that others often overlook.

_3_ 7. I do not shy away from putting a person on the spot when it seems necessary.

_2_ 8. I tend to be analytical.

_2_ 9. I often identify with others by using phrases like "I used to think that too" or "I once felt the way you do."

EVANGELISM STYLES QUESTIONNAIRE

___3___ 10. Other people have commented about my ability for developing new friendships.

___∅___ 11. To be honest, even if I know the answers, I am more comfortable having someone "better qualified" explain Christianity to my friends.

___1___ 12. I find fulfillment in helping others, often in behind-the-scenes ways.

___3___ 13. I do not have a problem confronting my friends with the truth even if it risks hurting the relationship.

___2___ 14. In conversations, I naturally focus on the questions that are holding up a person's spiritual progress.

___1___ 15. When I tell people of how I came to Christ, I have found that they have been interested in hearing it.

___2___ 16. I would rather delve into personal life issues than abstract theological ideas.

___2___ 17. If I knew of a high quality outreach event that my friends would enjoy, I would make a big effort to bring them.

___2___ 18. I prefer to show love through my actions more than my words.

___3___ 19. I believe that real love often means telling someone the truth, even when it hurts.

___1___ 20. I enjoy discussions and debates on difficult questions.

___3___ 21. I intentionally share my mistakes with others when it will help them relate to the solutions I have found.

EVANGELISM STYLES QUESTIONNAIRE

_1_ 22. I prefer getting involved in discussions concerning a person's life before dealing with the details of their beliefs.

_1_ 23. I tend to watch for spiritually strategic events to bring people to (such as Christian concerts, outreach events, seeker services).

_2_ 24. When people are spiritually closed, I have found that my quiet demonstrations of Christian love sometimes make them more receptive.

_2_ 25. A motto that would fit me is: "Make a difference or a mess, but do something."

_2_ 26. I often get frustrated with people when they use weak arguments or poor logic.

_2_ 27. People seem interested in hearing stories about things that have happened in my life.

_3_ 28. I enjoy long talks with friends.

_1_ 29. I am always looking for a match between the needs and interests of my friends and the various events, books, etc., that they would enjoy or benefit from.

_1_ 30. I feel more comfortable physically assisting a person in the name of Christ than getting involved in religious discussions.

_2_ 31. I sometimes get in trouble for lacking gentleness and sensitivity in the way I interact with others.

_3_ 32. I like to get at the underlying reasons for opinions that people hold.

EVANGELISM STYLES QUESTIONNAIRE

_1_ 33. I am still amazed at how God brought me to faith in Him and I am motivated to tell people about it.

_2_ 34. People generally consider me to be an interactive, sensitive, and caring kind of person.

_2_ 35. A highlight of my week would be to take a guest with me to an appropriate church event.

_2_ 36. I tend to be more practical and action-oriented than philosophical and idea-oriented.

	Confrontational	Intellectual	Testimonial	Interpersonal	Invitational	Serving
	#1 _3_	#2 _1_	#3 _3_	#4 _2_	#5 _3_	#6 _1_
	#7 _3_	#8 _2_	#9 _2_	#10 _3_	#11 _∅_	#12 _1_
	#13 _3_	#14 _2_	#15 _1_	#16 _2_	#17 _2_	#18 _2_
	#19 _3_	#20 _1_	#21 _3_	#22 _1_	#23 _1_	#24 _2_
	#25 _2_	#26 _2_	#27 _2_	#28 _3_	#29 _1_	#30 _1_
	#31 _2_	#32 _3_	#33 _1_	#34 _2_	#35 _2_	#36 _2_
TOTALS	16	11	12	13	9	9

Being
Yourself

In Session 2 you will:

1. Identify your style of evangelism

2. Identify a step to develop it

3. Clarify your understanding of others' Evangelism Styles

SIX STYLES OF EVANGELISM

CONFRONTATIONAL STYLE

Acts 2

Biblical Example:  Peter

Characteristics:

- Confident

- Assertive

- Direct

Contemporary Examples:

- Billy Graham

- Chuck Colson

Cautions:

Be sure to use tact when confronting people with truth to keep them from becoming unnecessarily offended.

SIX STYLES OF EVANGELISM

INTELLECTUAL STYLE

Acts 17

Biblical Example: *Paul*

Characteristics:

- Inquisitive

- Analytical

- _____

Contemporary Examples:

- Josh McDowell

- D. James Kennedy

Cautions:

Do not substitute giving answers for giving the Gospel message, and be careful of becoming argumentative.

SIX STYLES OF EVANGELISM

TESTIMONIAL STYLE *Experience / Examples*

Biblical Example: Blind Man John 9

Characteristics:

- Clear communicator

- Story teller

- Good listener

Contemporary Examples:

- Corrie ten Boom

- Joni Erickson Tada

Cautions:

Beware of talking about yourself but not relating your experience to the other person's life. You first need to *listen* to them to be able to connect your story to their situation.

SIX STYLES OF EVANGELISM

INTERPERSONAL STYLE Relationships

Biblical Example: Matthew Lk 5:29

Characteristics:

- Warm personality

- Conversational

- Friendship oriented

Contemporary Examples:

- Becky Pippert

- Joe Aldrich

Cautions:

Avoid valuing friendship over truth-telling. Presenting the Gospel often means challenging a person's whole direction in life, and that can mean causing friction in your relationship.

SIX STYLES OF EVANGELISM

INVITATIONAL STYLE   *Interest of others*

Biblical Example: _Woman at Well_
John 4

Characteristics:

- Hospitable

- Relational

- _Persasive_

Contemporary Example:

- Ruth Graham

Cautions:

Be careful not to always let others do your talking for you. You, too, need to "always be prepared to give an answer to everyone who asks you to give the reason for the hope that you have ..." (1 Peter 3:15).

SIX STYLES OF EVANGELISM

SERVING STYLE *Needs of others*
Uses skills

Biblical Example: *Dorcas   Acts 9*

Characteristics:

- Others-centered

- Humble

- *Very patient*

Contemporary Examples:

- Mother Teresa

- Jimmy Carter

Cautions:

Just as "words are no substitute for actions," "actions are no substitute for words." In Romans 10:14, it is made clear that we must *verbally* tell people about Christ.

ACTIVITY: EVANGELISM STYLES ASSESSMENT

The following reference material provides some additional information on each Evangelism Style. Individuals with a particular Evangelism Style typically evidence certain traits, some of which are listed. You may find these helpful in better understanding or confirming your Evangelism Style.

DIRECTIONS

1. Locate in the *Evangelism Styles Assessment* what you have identified as your primary style of evangelism.

2. As you read through the information about your Evangelism Style, check any item you feel applies to you. If you begin to sense that the items are not particularly descriptive of you, take a look at the style that had the second highest total on your *Evangelism Styles Questionnaire*. See if that may be a better match.

3. Identify one idea to begin developing your style.

4. Write your style(s) on your *Impact List* on the inside back cover of your Participant's Guide.

Note: Do not let it confuse you if you scored high in more than one style. This may be an indication that you can work through multiple styles, depending on the particular need. Also, as you try these different styles, one or two may emerge as stronger than the others.

EVANGELISM STYLES ASSESSMENT

CONFRONTATIONAL STYLE

Biblical Example: Peter in Acts 2

Theme Verse: 2 Timothy 4:2

Preach the Word; be prepared in season and out of season; correct, rebuke and encourage—with great patience and careful instruction.

Contemporary Examples: Chuck Colson, Billy Graham

Traits:
❑ Confident
❑ Bold
❑ Direct
❑ Skips small talk, likes to get right to the point
❑ Has strong opinions and convictions

Cautions:
• Be sure to seek God's wisdom so you will be appropriately sensitive and tactful.
• Allow the Holy Spirit to restrain your desire to come on strong in every situation.
• Avoid judging or laying guilt trips on others who approach evangelism with a different style.

Suggestions for Using and Developing this Style:
❑ Ask friends for feedback on whether or not you have the right balance of boldness and gentleness. Keep in mind Paul's phrase in Ephesians 4, "speaking the truth in love." Both truth and love are essential.
❑ Prepare yourself for situations where you will stand alone (read about Peter in Acts 2 and other scripture). The non-believer you confront with the truth will sometimes feel uncomfortable. Even non-confrontational Christians who are with you will sometimes feel that discomfort. That's okay. Under God's guidance challenge people to trust and follow Christ, and He will use it.

EVANGELISM STYLES ASSESSMENT

❑ Practice the principle of "Putting Others First." It is critical that you listen and value what others say before telling them what you think they need to hear.

❑ Team up with friends who have other styles that may be better matched to the personality of the person you hope to reach.

❑ Other: _____

INTELLECTUAL STYLE

Biblical Example: Paul in Acts 17

Theme Verse: 2 Corinthians 10:5

We demolish arguments and every pretension that sets itself up against the knowledge of God, and we take captive every thought to make it obedient to Christ.

Contemporary Examples: Josh McDowell, D. James Kennedy

Traits:
❑ Analytical
❑ Logical
❑ Inquisitive
❑ Likes to debate
❑ More concerned with what people think than what they feel

Cautions:
• Avoid getting stuck on academic points, arguments, and evidence. These are mainly to clear the way back to the central Gospel message.
• Remember that attitude is as important as information. 1 Peter 3:15 says to have "gentleness and respect."
• Avoid becoming argumentative.

EVANGELISM STYLES ASSESSMENT

Suggestions for Using and Developing this Style:

❑ Set time aside to study and prepare. This style, more than the others, relies on preparation. Take serious action on what it says in 1 Peter 3:15:

> *But in your hearts set apart Christ as Lord. Always be prepared to give an answer to everyone who asks you to give the reason for the hope that you have. But do this with gentleness and respect.*

❑ Avoid doing all your preparation in an academic vacuum. Get out and talk to others. Try out your arguments and answers on real people, and make refinements as needed.

❑ Develop your relational side. Talk to people about everyday events, and what is happening in their life and yours.

❑ Team up with friends who have other styles that may be better matched to the personality of the person you hope to reach.

❑ Other: _____

TESTIMONIAL STYLE

Biblical Example: The Blind Man in John 9

Theme Verse: 1 John 1:3a

> *We proclaim to you what we have seen and heard, so that you also may have fellowship with us . . .*

Contemporary Examples: Corrie ten Boom, Joni Erickson Tada

Traits:

❑ Clear communicator
❑ Good listener
❑ Vulnerable about personal life, its ups and downs
❑ Overwhelmed by the account of how God reached them
❑ Sees links between their own experience and that of other people's

29

EVANGELISM STYLES ASSESSMENT

Cautions:

- Be sure to relate your experience to the life of your listener. This requires first hearing enough about your friend's life to know how to relate your story to their situation.
- Do not stop with merely telling your story. Challenge them to consider how what you learned might apply to their life.
- Avoid downplaying the value of your story because it seems too ordinary. The ordinary story is the kind that relates best to ordinary people!

Suggestions for Using and Developing this Style:

- ❏ Practice so you will be able to tell your story without hesitation.
- ❏ Keep Christ and the Gospel message as the centerpiece of your story. This is an account of how He changed your life.
- ❏ Keep your story fresh by adding new and current illustrations from your daily walk with Christ.
- ❏ Team up with friends who have other styles that may be better matched to the personality of the person you hope to reach.

- ❏ Other: _____

INTERPERSONAL STYLE

Biblical Example: Matthew in Luke 5

Theme Verse: 1 Corinthians 9:22

> *. . . I have become all things to all men so that by all possible means I might save some.*

Contemporary Examples: Becky Pippert, Joe Aldrich

EVANGELISM STYLES ASSESSMENT

Traits:
- ❏ Conversational
- ❏ Compassionate
- ❏ Sensitive
- ❏ Friendship-oriented
- ❏ Focuses on people and their needs

Cautions:
- • Beware of valuing friendship over truth. Telling them they are sinners in need of a savior will test the relationship.
- • Do not get so involved in the process of building friendships that you forget the ultimate goal: bringing people to know Christ as forgiver and leader.
- • Do not get overwhelmed with the amount of needs your friends might have—do what you can and leave the rest to God.

Suggestions for Using and Developing this Style:
- ❏ Be patient. This style tends to work more gradually than others. Look and pray for opportunities to turn conversations toward spiritual matters.
- ❏ Continually create and plan opportunities to interact with new people through social events, sports, etc. This will put you in a position where your style can flourish.
- ❏ Practice telling the Gospel message so you will be prepared when the opportunity arises.
- ❏ Team up with friends who have other styles that may be better matched to the personality of the person you hope to reach.
- ❏ Other: _____

EVANGELISM STYLES ASSESSMENT

INVITATIONAL STYLE

Biblical Example: The woman at the well in John 4.

Theme Verse: Luke 14:23

Then the master told his servant, "Go out to the roads and country lanes and make them come in, so that my house will be full."

Contemporary Example: Ruth Graham

Traits:
- ❑ Hospitable
- ❑ Persuasive
- ❑ Enjoys meeting new people
- ❑ Committed (believes in the things in which he or she is involved)
- ❑ Sees outreach events as unique opportunities

Cautions:
- Do not let others do *all* the talking for you. Your friends and acquaintances need to hear how Christ has influenced your own life. In addition, your friends have questions you could answer concerning the implications of the Gospel in their own lives.
- Carefully and prayerfully consider which events or church services you take people to. Look for ones that are truly sensitive to spiritual seekers that will help them in their journey toward Christ.
- Do not get discouraged if people refuse your invitation. Their refusal could be an opportunity for a spiritual conversation. Also, their "no" today may be a "yes" tomorrow.

Suggestions for Using and Developing this Style:
- ❑ When inviting people, try to get written details about the event into their hands (either preprinted or handwritten out). Whenever appropriate, offer to pick them up and do something together before or after the event.

EVANGELISM STYLES ASSESSMENT

❑ At events, put yourself in the place of the other person. Ask yourself if you were that person, whether the event would relate to your concerns and mindset. Reinforce those things to the person you invited.

❑ Offer positive and constructive feedback to the event sponsors consisting of specific and realistic ideas on ways you think they could improve the event and make it more compelling to the people you bring.

❑ Team up with friends who have other styles that may be better matched to the personality of the person you hope to reach.

❑ Other: _____

SERVING STYLE

Biblical Example: Dorcas in Acts 9

Theme Verse: Matthew 5:16

In the same way, let your light shine before men, that they may see your good deeds and praise your Father in heaven.

Contemporary Examples: Mother Teresa, Jimmy Carter

Traits:
❑ Patient
❑ Others-centered
❑ Sees needs and finds joy in meeting them
❑ Shows love through action more than words
❑ Attaches value to even menial tasks

EVANGELISM STYLES ASSESSMENT

Cautions:

- Remember that although "words are no substitute for actions," "actions are no substitute for words." In Romans 10:14 Paul says that we must verbally tell people about Christ. You can do this in many ways as you point to Him as the central motivation for your acts of service.
- Do not underestimate the value of your service. It is your style that will reach those persons who are the most negative and hardened toward God. Acts of loving service are hard to resist and difficult to argue with.
- Be discerning as to how much you can do realistically, without depriving yourself or your family of needed care and attention.

Suggestions for Using and Developing this Style:

❑ Find creative, non-imposing ways to communicate the spiritual motivation behind the physical acts of service you offer to others. It could be through a word, a card, an invitation in response to thanks for your service. ("Well, one thing you could do for me sometime would be to come to one of our services at church.")

❑ Seek God daily for opportunities to serve others for eternal purposes. He will open your eyes to areas you would have missed. Be ready to follow His leadings, even if they seem a bit out of the ordinary.

❑ Be careful not to impose your service on others. Pray for wisdom so you will know where to invest your efforts in ways that will be strategic for the Kingdom of God.

❑ Team up with friends who have other styles that may be better matched to the personality of the person you hope to reach.

❑ Other: _____

HUDDLE GROUP: EVANGELISM STYLES

DIRECTIONS

Form a huddle group with three other people.

1. Using the *Evangelism Styles Assessment,* further clarify
   your Evangelism Style by sharing with your group:

   a. Your Evangelism Style, and why you think it fits you

   b. Cautions you think you need to be aware of with
      your style

   c. One idea to develop your style

2. Listen to the others in your group to get a better understanding of other Evangelism Styles.

3. Select someone to keep track of the time, so that everyone
   gets a turn.

SESSION SUMMARY

In this session you:

- Identified your Evangelism Style

- Identified steps to develop your styles

- Clarified your understanding of others' Evangelism Styles

SUGGESTED READING: CHAPTER 9

(*Becoming a Contagious Christian* companion book)

To further explore how you can reach others by being yourself, we encourage you to read Chapter 9, titled "Finding an Approach that Fits You." It will expand your understanding of your own style of evangelism.

Building Relationships *w/ those outside the church*

O V E R V I E W

In Session 3 you will:

1. Identify how to initiate relationships

2. Identify methods for starting spiritual conversations

3. Write down statements for transitioning into a spiritual conversation

BUILDING RELATIONSHIPS

PEOPLE WE _Already_ **KNOW**

Suggestions:

- Include them in activities we are _doing_
- Organize a _Matthew party_
- _Bar-b-que_ First!

PEOPLE WE _Used_ **TO KNOW**

PEOPLE WE WOULD _Like_ **TO KNOW**

Suggestion:

- Strategic _Consumerism_   _no pay at pump_
  see people face to face

POINTS TO REMEMBER

- _Pray_
- _Listen_
- Build on areas of _Common ground_
- Mention spiritual matters _early_ :)

STARTING SPIRITUAL CONVERSATIONS

THREE METHODS

Direct Method—Typically takes the form of a question or statement:

- Do you ever think about _Spiritual matters_ ?
- Where do you think you are on your spiritual _journey_ ?—Joseph Aldrich
- If you ever want to know the difference between religion and Christianity, let me know.—Bill Hybels

Indirect Method

- Builds on the direction the conversation is already heading by using the topic being discussed as a _bridge_ to a related *spiritual* topic

Invitational Method

- Transitions the conversation by inviting your friend to a Christian event that relates to the topic you are discussing

Tips for inviting people:

- Offer to pick them up
- Do something before or after the event

EXERCISE: STARTING SPIRITUAL CONVERSATIONS

DIRECTIONS

The scenario is you having a conversation with a non-believing friend, co-worker, or family member—preferably someone from your *Impact List* on page 11.

1. Read each situation.

2. Write down a statement or question you would *say* to transition the conversation to a spiritual one. Use the Indirect or Invitational method.

3. Complete as many as possible in the time allowed.

EXERCISE: STARTING SPIRITUAL CONVERSATIONS

Situation	Possible Transitions
1. You are in a situation where it is natural to comment on the beautiful weather, spectacular sights, intricacies of nature, or the wonder of creation (for example—you are hiking or at the zoo). Sample Transition: "God must have quite an imagination to create such beauty."	You would say: "
2. Your friend has just told you about the hobbies they like doing in their spare time, and they are interested in knowing about yours. Sample Transition: "I enjoy spending my spare time building into the lives of the Junior High kids at our church."	You would say: "
3. You are talking with a work associate about an upcoming holiday like Thanksgiving, Christmas, or Easter. Sample Transition: "I'm curious, do you observe any family or religious traditions around the holiday?"	You would say: "

EXERCISE: STARTING SPIRITUAL CONVERSATIONS

Situation	Possible Transitions
4. You are with some friends, talking about the latest TV show, news program, or song. Sample Transition: "Another song I enjoy on the radio is _____ by _____, a singer who is a Christian, and really has a lot to say."	You would say: "
5. It is the close of the football/baseball/basketball season, the playoffs are in full swing, and everybody is watching and talking about the event. Sample Transition: "One of the things I enjoy most about the sport is watching _____. He obviously plays well, but, as a Christian, he seems to bring a different attitude to the game."	You would say: "
6. Your friend confides in you about a problem they are facing or a difficulty they are working through. Sample Transition: "I can relate to the problem you're describing. I've struggled with it too, but what made a marked difference was when I discovered a source of spiritual strength ..."	You would say: "

PRINCIPLES FOR STARTING SPIRITUAL CONVERSATIONS

- Focus on the other person's _____ interests

  and ___Concerns___

- Be willing to take ___risks___

- Make the most of split-second ___opportunities___

Remember—Put Others First!

INDIVIDUAL EXERCISE: *UPDATE YOUR IMPACT LIST*

DIRECTIONS

1. Review the names you listed on page 11 in your Participant's Guide to see if those are the people you still feel God is asking you to develop friendships with. Then write 1 to 3 of those names on your *Impact List* located on the inside back cover of your Participant's Guide.

2. Identify where they are on the *Readiness Scale* (located across from your *Impact List*) and mark their level next to their name.

3. Update the following information for the *#1 person* on your *Impact List:*

    a. List areas of common ground that you have with them.

    b. Review the transition statement you wrote down (pages 41–42); write one or two that would be effective with that person.

    c. Determine the next step to take with that person relationally and spiritually. You might want to review the *Readiness Scale* (across from the inside back cover) and the sample completed *Impact List* for ideas.

4. Later, do the same for the other people on your *Impact List.*

Note: There is a sample completed *Impact List* on the next page.

Impact List   Name: _Joe T. Sample_   Style: _Interpersonal_

The names of your *Impact List* will change as they become Christians or move out of your sphere of influence. This list should be an ongoing part of your evangelism strategy.

Remember to develop "no-strings-attached" friendships with these people. Let them know by word and action that they matter to you, regardless of whether or not they agree with the Christian message.

Name	Level of Readiness (1–4)	Areas of Common Ground	Conversational Transitions	Next Steps Relationally	Next Steps Spiritually
Jeff	2 (spectator)	• Same line of work • Kids the same age • Both play tennis	"Jeff, I read a book recently on parenting from a Christian perspective . . . thought you'd find it interesting."	1. Meet for lunch 2. Play tennis 3. Do something with combined families	1. Raise spiritual topics 2. Give book on parenting 3. Invite to church
Steve	3 (skeptic)	• Neighbor • Similar music tastes • Both like to debate issues	"Steve, I understand why you distrust organized religion. I've often felt the same way . . ."	1. Spend more time together (earn trust) 2. Help him build deck 3. Invite over for a meal	1. Tell him my story 2. Research his questions 3. Invite to appropriate concert
Betty	2 (spectator)	• Family member • Same religious background • Both like hikes	"When you look at all this beautiful scenery, Betty, does it ever make you think how much we must matter to the one who made it all?"	1. Call more often 2. Keep her up-to-date with my kids 3. Deepen conversations to more personal level	1. Help her see the difference between going to church and have a relationship with Christ

SESSION SUMMARY

In this session you:

- Identified how to initiate relationships

- Identified methods for starting spiritual conversations

- Wrote down statements for transitioning into a spiritual conversation

---

SUGGESTED READING: CHAPTERS 7, 8, 10

(*Becoming a Contagious Christian* companion book)

To reinforce your understanding of relationship-building, read chapters 7, 8, and 10.

Chapter 7 is titled "Strategic Opportunities in Relationships," and Chapter 8, "Rubbing Shoulders with Irreligious People." In addition, Chapter 10, "Starting Spiritual Conversations," lists numerous ideas you might find helpful for turning conversations toward matters of faith.

What's Your Story?

In this session you will:

1. Identify why your story is important

2. Write out your personal story

3. Practice telling your story in a safe environment

WHY YOUR STORY IS IMPORTANT

- Our friends are ___interested___

- Our friends can ___relate___ to it

- It is ___hard to refute___

HOW TO ORGANIZE YOUR STORY

PAUL'S STORY—ACTS 26: THE THREE HANDLES

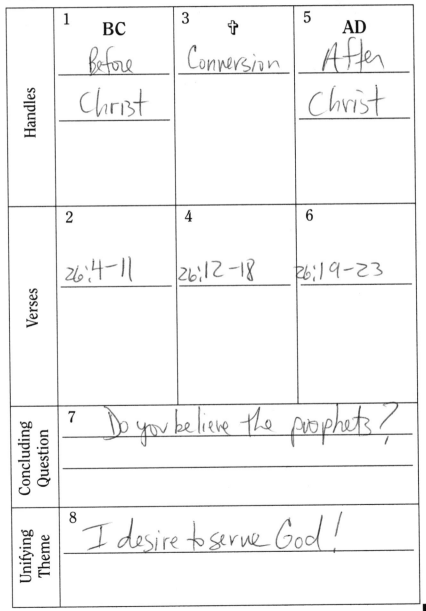

	1 **BC**	3 ✝	5 **AD**
Handles	Before Christ	Conversion	After Christ
Verses	2 26:4-11	4 26:12-18	6 26:19-23
Concluding Question	7 Do you believe the prophets?		
Unifying Theme	8 I desire to serve God!		

Use current events in your life?

WRITING YOUR STORY

BC—BEFORE CHRIST

	Outline
1. Where were you spiritually before receiving Christ, and how did that affect you—your feelings, attitudes, actions, and relationships?* *As I grew up, my mom had a lot of fears and insecurities that were passed on to me. As a result, I did not feel like I could trust anyone, including God.* * If you became a Christian as a child you can start with question #2.	
2. What caused you to begin considering God/Christ as a solution to your needs? *When I was in college, my roommate invited me to her church where the minister explained that most people try to find security in other people or things. But he said only God could give us the security that we are looking for.*	

WRITING YOUR STORY

✝—CONVERSION

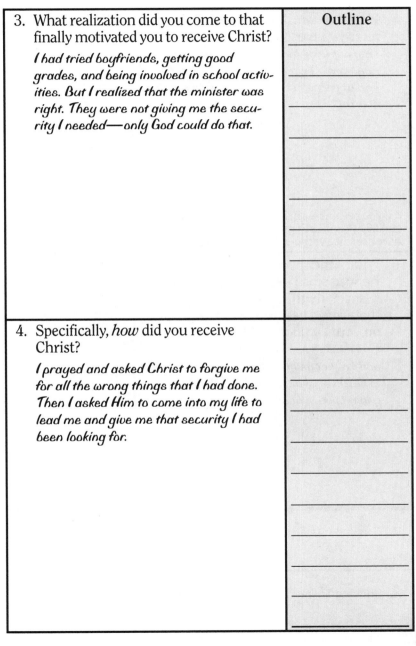

	Outline
3. What realization did you come to that finally motivated you to receive Christ? *I had tried boyfriends, getting good grades, and being involved in school activities. But I realized that the minister was right. They were not giving me the security I needed—only God could do that.*	_____ _____ _____ _____ _____ _____ _____ _____ _____ _____
4. Specifically, *how* did you receive Christ? *I prayed and asked Christ to forgive me for all the wrong things that I had done. Then I asked Him to come into my life to lead me and give me that security I had been looking for.*	_____ _____ _____ _____ _____ _____ _____ _____ _____

WRITING YOUR STORY

AD—AFTER CONVERSION

	Outline
5. How did your life begin to change after you trusted Christ?* *I did not have that fear and insecurity anymore. I began to feel more confident and at peace because I knew God was in control.*	
Here and now —	
* If you became a Christian as a child, answer #5 and #6 by contrasting your life to what it might have been like without Christ (see below).	
6. What other benefits have you experienced since becoming a Christian? (Especially think of those benefits that would best relate to the people on your *Impact List*.) *I have much healthier relationships now, and I'm not as afraid of failing as I used to be. Most of all, I now know that I am going to be in heaven for eternity!*	
7. Concluding Question: *Can you relate to any of this?*	
8. Unifying Theme: *Looking for security.*	

* This can be determined by reflecting on eras of your life when you weren't close to Him, by considering your areas of weakness and temptation, and/or by observing the lifestyles chosen by old friends or schoolmates who *didn't* follow Christ.

STORY TIPS

THEME

- The central issue in our lives that shows the _Contrast_ in our spiritual outlook before and after knowing Christ

MIDDLE HANDLE

- We need to keep it simple, clear, and _repeatable_

CONCLUSION

- End with a question or statement that requires a _response / choice_

SCRIPTURE

John 10:10

- Think of whether there was one key verse that really opened your eyes. If not, do not force it.

LANGUAGE _lost, repent, (sin)_

- Avoid religious clichés and "God-talk"

Define your terms !
Far from God –
Christ-followers –

LENGTH

- Be _brief_ and to the point

SEQUENCE

- With practice you will be able to start and end at any one of the handles, depending on the situation

PUTTING OTHERS FIRST

- Keep your focus on your friend
- Emphasize those aspects of your story that will relate to *his or her* concerns and interests

INDIVIDUAL EXERCISE: OUTLINE YOUR STORY

DIRECTIONS

1. Refer back to your answers to the six questions, and circle the key words in each of your answers.

2. Write those key words in outline form in the space provided in the column to the right of your answers to the six questions. A sample is provided on pages 55–56.

> This is just a *first draft*. You will have plenty of time, in fact the rest of your life, to polish your story.

INDIVIDUAL EXERCISE: OUTLINE YOUR STORY

WRITING YOUR STORY—SAMPLE

		Outline
BC	1. Where were you spiritually before receiving Christ, and how did that affect you—your feelings, attitudes, actions, and relationships? *As I grew up, my (mom) had a lot of (fears) and (insecurities) that were passed on to me. As a result, I did (not feel) like I could (trust anyone,) including (God.)*	Mom's fears and insecurities Couldn't trust anyone Even God
	2. What caused you to begin considering God/Christ as a solution to your needs? *When I was in (college,) my (roommate) invited me to (her church) where the minister explained that most people try to find (security in other) people or things. But he said (only God could give) us the (security) that we are looking for.*	College Roommate her church Security in others Only God gives security
✝	3. What realization did you come to that finally motivated you to receive Christ? *I had (tried) boyfriends, getting good grades, and being involved in school activities. But I realized that the (minister was right.) They were not giving me the (security) I needed—(only God) could do that.*	Tried everything Minister right Only God gives security
	4. Specifically, *how* did you receive Christ? *I (prayed) and asked Christ to (forgive me) for all the wrong things that I had done. Then I asked Him to come into my life to (lead me) and (give me that security) I had been looking for.*	Prayed Forgive me Lead me Give me security

INDIVIDUAL EXERCISE: OUTLINE YOUR STORY

WRITING YOUR STORY—SAMPLE, con't.

AD		Outline
	5. How did your life begin to change after you trusted Christ? *I did not have that fear and insecurity anymore. I began to feel more confident and at peace because I knew God was in control.*	**Outline** *No more fear* *and insecurity* *More confident, peaceful* *God was in control*
	6. What other benefits have you experienced since becoming a Christian? (Especially think of those benefits that would best relate to the people on your *Impact List*.) *I have much healthier relationships now, and also I'm not as afraid of failing as I used to be. Most of all, I now know that I am going to be in heaven for eternity!*	*Healthier relationships* *Less fear of failure* *Heaven!*
	7. Concluding Question: *Can you relate to any of this?*	*Can you relate?*
	8. Unifying Theme: *Looking for security.*	

PARTNER ACTIVITY: PRACTICE TELLING YOUR STORY

DIRECTIONS

1. Get with a partner. One of you tell your story, the other use the *Story Feedback Checklist* to write down any comments.

2. After the first person has told his or her story, the listener provides verbal feedback on what worked well, and what areas could be improved. (Use the checklist to guide you.)

3. Then trade places, the listener becomes the teller, the teller becomes the listener. Repeat steps one and two.

Story Feedback Checklist

ITEM	OBSERVATIONS
Three Handles: ☐ BC—clearly explained ☐ ✝ —was repeatable ☐ AD—clearly explained	What worked well?
☐ **Theme**—resolved a central idea ☐ **Conclusion**—asked for a response ☐ **Scripture**—did not overuse ☐ **Language**—avoided religious clichés (If not, what were they?) ☐ **Length**—was within four minutes	**Areas for Improvement:**

. SESSION SUMMARY

In this session you:

- Identified why your story is important

- Wrote your personal story using the three handles

- Practiced telling your story

SUGGESTED READING: NONE

What's His Story?

In Session 5 you will:

1. Identify the four major points of the Gospel message

2. Practice presenting two Gospel illustrations

THE GOSPEL MESSAGE

1. _____GOD_____

a. God is ___love___.

> ... *God is love. Whoever lives in love lives in God, and God in him (1 John 4:16b).*

b. God is ___holy___ (absolutely pure).

> *But just as he who called you is holy, so be holy in all you do; for it is written: "Be holy, because I am holy" (1 Peter 1:16).*

✴ c. God is ___just___ (a good judge).

> *God is just: He will pay back trouble to those who trouble you (2 Thessalonians 1:6).*

THE GOSPEL MESSAGE

2. _____U$_____

a. We were created good, but became ___*sinful*___.

   For all have sinned and fall short of the glory of God (Romans 3:23).

b. We deserve ___*death*___ (physical & spiritual).

   For the wages of sin is death . . . (Romans 6:23).

   (See also Hebrews 9:22)

✗ c. We are spiritually ___*helpless*___ ("morally bankrupt").

   All of us have become like one who is unclean, and all our righteous acts are like filthy rags . . . (Isaiah 64:6).

   (See also Ephesians 2:8–9)

no works, no money will be enough

THE GOSPEL MESSAGE

3. _JEU /Christ_

a. Christ is _____God_____, who also became man.

In the beginning was the Word, and the Word was with God, and the Word was God . . . . The Word became flesh and made his dwelling among us. We have seen his glory, the glory of the One and Only, who came from the Father, full of grace and truth (John 1:1,14).

(See also John 8:24)

b. Christ died as our _____substitute_____.

He himself bore our sins in his body on the tree, so that we might die to sins and live for righteousness; by his wounds you have been healed (1 Peter 2:24).

(See also 1 Peter 3:18; 2 Corinthians 5:21)

✳ c. Christ offers His forgiveness as a _____gift_____.

For it is by grace you have been saved, through faith— and this not from yourselves, it is the gift of God—not by works, so that no one can boast (Ephesians 2:8–9).

(See also Romans 6:23)

THE GOSPEL MESSAGE

4. _____You_____

a. You and I must ___respond___.

Yet to all who received him, to those who believed in his name, he gave the right to become children of God. (John 1:12).

(See also Romans 10:13)

b. We must ask Christ to be our ___forgiver___ and ___leader___.

If we confess our sins, he is faithful and just and will forgive us our sins and purify us from all unrighteousness (1 John 1:9).

But in your hearts set apart Christ as Lord . . . (1 Peter 3:15).

(See also John 10:27; Luke 13:5)

c. The result is a spiritual ___transformation___ by the Holy Spirit.

Therefore, if anyone is in Christ, he is a new creation; the old has gone, the new has come! (2 Corinthians 5:17).

(See also 1 Corinthians 6:19–20)

PRESENTING THE GOSPEL

Do vs. Done

This illustration is a natural follow-up to the question "Would you like to know the difference between religion and Christianity?"

Narrative	Outline
The difference between religion and Christianity is: Religion is spelled "D-O." It consists of trying to do enough good things to somehow please God, earn His forgiveness, and gain entrance into heaven. This self-effort plan can take on many forms, from trying to be a good, moral person, to becoming an active participant in an organized religion —Christian or otherwise.	**Religion** • Is spelled "D-O" • Trying to do enough good things to please God
The problem is, we can never know when we have done enough. Even worse, the Bible makes it clear that we can *never* do enough in Romans 3:23: "For all have sinned and fall short of the glory of God." Simply put, the "D-O" plan cannot bring us peace with God, or even peace with ourselves.	**The Problem** • We can never know when we have done enough • The Bible says that *we* can *never* do enough (Romans 3:23)
Christianity, however, is spelled "D-O-N-E." In other words, that which we could never *do* for ourselves, Christ has already *done* for us. He lived the perfect life we could never live, and He died on the cross to pay for each of our wrongdoings. And now He freely offers us His gift of forgiveness and leadership for our lives.	**Christianity** • Is spelled "D-O-N-E" • Christ did what we could never do —Lived the perfect life we could not —Died on the cross to pay for our wrongdoings
But, it's not enough just to know this, we have to humbly receive what He has done for us. And we do that by asking for His forgiveness and leadership in our lives.	**Our Response** • It's not enough just to know this • We have to *receive* what He has done for us • By asking for His forgiveness and leadership in our lives
[At this point, ask them a follow-up question like: "Does this make sense to you?" or "What do you think about what I just said?"]	**Their Response** • Does this make sense to you? • What do you think about what I just said?

PRESENTING THE GOSPEL

The Bridge

The Bridge uses a simple drawing to illustrate the Gospel message.*

Narrative	Outline	Picture
We matter to God. He made us, and He wants to have a relationship with us. *[Write "us" on one side of a piece of paper and "God" on the other.]*	God wants to have a relationship with us.	
However, we have rebelled against God, we have all disobeyed Him, our sins have separated us from Him and broken off the relationship. *[Draw lines by both words in such a way that they form walls around a large chasm, separating us from God.]*	However, we have rebelled against Him and broken off that relationship.	
To varying degrees, most of us are aware of our distance from God, so we start doing all kinds of things like being a helpful neighbor, paying our taxes, going to church, or giving money to charities—all in order to get back to Him. There is nothing wrong with these things, but the Bible makes it clear that none of them can earn us God's forgiveness or reestablish our relationship with Him. *[Draw arrows going over the "Us" cliff. These signify our attempts to reach God that always fall short. Optional: Write "Romans 3:23" next to the arrows so the person can see the biblical source for the illustration.]*	Most of us are aware of this and try to *do* things to get back to God, but it doesn't work.	

PRESENTING THE GOSPEL

The Bridge, continued

Narrative	Outline	Picture
Furthermore, the sins we have committed must be punished. The penalty we owe is death, which is a physical death as well as a spiritual separation from God for eternity in a place called hell. *[Add the word "Death" at the bottom of the chasm. Optional: Write "Romans 6:23" next to the word "Death."]*	Furthermore, the sins we have committed have to be punished, and that punishment is death.	
It looks pretty bleak, but the good news is that we matter to God. In fact, He loves us so much that He did for us what we could never do for ourselves. He provided a bridge over which we can find His forgiveness and restore our relationship with him. *[Draw a cross so it touches both sides of the chasm. Optional: Add "1 Peter 3:18" next to the cross.]*	*But* God did for us what we could not do, and that is build a bridge back to Himself.	
He built it by coming to earth as one of us and dying on the cross to pay the death penalty we owed. *[X out the word "Death"]* This is a picture of what the central message of the Bible is all about. This is what God wants each of us to understand. But it is not enough for us to just know about this, or even agree with it. We have to act on it. God wants us to move over to the other side. We do this by humbly admitting to God that we have rebelled against Him, and that we need his forgiveness and leadership. With our sins pardoned and our debt paid, our relationship with God is firmly established because we are immediately	And He did that by paying our death penalty when He died on the cross. One last thing. It is not enough just to know this, we have to *act* on it by admitting that we have rebelled, and that we want His forgiveness and leadership.	

PRESENTING THE GOSPEL

The Bridge, continued

Narrative	Outline	Picture
adopted into His family as His son or daughter. *[While explaining this, draw a stick figure on the "Us" side of the chasm, then an arrow from the stick figure to the "God" side of the chasm, then another figure on the "God" side of the chasm. Optional: Add "John 1:12."]* *[At this point, ask them if the illustration makes sense to them, or if there is any part of it that they would like to discuss. Finally, ask them where they are on the drawing and, if they seem open, whether they would like to move over the bridge by making Christ their forgiver, leader, and friend.]* *[Note: If they are not ready it may be helpful to write in the 4 verses mentioned above, and give them the diagram to study and think about.]*	Concluding Questions: • *Does this make sense to you?* • *Where do you think you are?* • *Is there any reason why you wouldn't want to cross over to the other side?*	

PRESENTING THE GOSPEL: YOUR CHOICE OF ILLUSTRATIONS

Here you will practice telling presenting the Gospel using either the Do vs. Done, or The Bridge illustration. You will practice telling it as though you were talking with the #1 person on your *Impact List*.

DIRECTIONS

1. Select a person on your *Impact List* and tell your partner this person's first name, the nature of your relationship (neighbor, relative, etc.), and where the person is on the *Readiness Scale*. This will help your partner interact with you as the person on your *Impact List* might interact.
2. Select and present the illustration (The Bridge, or Do vs. Done) that your *Impact List* person will best relate to. Partners, cooperate with the person presenting the illustration; do not try to make it difficult for them.
3. After the first person has presented their illustration, the listener provides feedback on what worked well and what areas could be improved. Use the form on the next page as your feedback checklist.
4. Then trade places. Repeat steps one and two.

Here are some pointers for your 1 minute debriefing:

- For the presenter, talk about what worked well and one thing you will do differently the next time you give the illustration.
- For the listener, tell what you think was the strongest point of the presentation and give one or two suggestions for improvement.

   Use the space below to draw The Bridge illustration:

PRESENTING THE GOSPEL: YOUR CHOICE OF ILLUSTRATIONS

GOSPEL ILLUSTRATION CHECKLIST

ITEM	OBSERVATIONS
Which illustration was used? ❏ Do vs. Done ❏ The Bridge **Were the following four points mentioned?** ❏ God ❏ Us ❏ Christ ❏ You	**What worked well?**
Other points: ❏ Was the presentation free of religious cliches; was it easily understood? ❏ Was what you needed to do clear to you by the end of the presentation? ❏ Was the presentation within the 3 minute time limit?	**Areas for Improvement:**

SESSION SUMMARY

In this session you:

- Identified the four points of the Gospel message

- Practiced presenting two Gospel illustrations

SUGGESTED READING: CHAPTER 11

(*Becoming a Contagious Christian* companion book)

For a helpful review of the critically important content of this session, read Chapter 11, "Making the Message Clear." It will build your confidence in your own mastery of the elements in the message of the gospel.

Crossing the Line

In Session 6 you will:

1. Practice telling your personal story

2. Identify the steps in leading a person "across the line" of faith

3. Practice praying with someone to receive Christ

PARTNER ACTIVITY: PRACTICE TELLING YOUR STORY

DIRECTIONS

Partner with someone you have not worked with before. To review your story, turn back to pages 50–52.

1. One of you tell your story to your partner as though your partner were the #1 person on your *Impact List*. Briefly (30 seconds) tell your partner this person's first name, the nature of your relationship (neighbor, co-worker, relative, etc.), and where the person is on the *Readiness Scale*. This will help your partner interact with you as the person on your *Impact List* might interact.

   Note: the person role-playing the friend generally should *cooperate* with you.

2. After the first person has told his or her story, the listener provides feedback on what worked well and what areas could be improved. Use page 73 in your Participant's Guide as your feedback checklist.

3. Then trade places. Repeat steps one and two.

PARTNER ACTIVITY: PRACTICE TELLING YOUR STORY

STORY FEEDBACK CHECKLIST

ITEM	OBSERVATIONS
Three Handles: ❏ BC—clearly explained ❏ ✝—was repeatable ❏ AD—clearly explained ❏ **Theme**—resolved a central idea ❏ **Conclusion**—asked for a response	**What worked well?**
❏ **Scripture**—did not overuse ❏ **Language**—avoided religious clichés (If not, what were they?) ❏ **Length**—Was within four minutes	**Areas for Improvement:**

CROSSING THE LINE

ASSESS READINESS

- Have you come to the point of _Trusting Christ_ , or are you still in the process of thinking it through?

- Where would you say you are _right now_ in that process?

- Is there any reason you wouldn't want to ask God for His

   forgiveness and _leadership_
   right now?

PRAY

- You pray together, with you guiding the prayer by

   prompting them

- Prompt them to:

   Ask for God's _forgiveness_

   Ask for God's _leadership_

- Give thanks _to God_

CROSSING THE LINE

CELEBRATE THEIR COMMITMENT

- Keep in mind that not everyone will react the same way

- What matters is that they took a step of faith, not that some specific feeling is evoked

- You may want to share Luke 15:10b:

    . . . there is rejoicing in the presence of the angels of God over one sinner who repents.

TAKE THE NEXT STEP

1. Help your friend to get involved with other Christians.

    - Go to church and worship

    - Develop Christian friendships, including becoming involved in a small group

2. Encourage your friend to __pray__.

3. Encourage your friend to read the Bible regularly.

4. Finally, encourage them on how to relate to __non-Christians__

VIDEO VIGNETTE & PRACTICE: CROSSING THE LINE

DIRECTIONS

Partner with someone you feel comfortable with.

1. Using page 77 as a guide, practice leading your partner "across the line" as though your partner were the #1 person on your *Impact List*. *Briefly* tell your partner the first name of your friend, the nature of your relationship (neighbor, co-worker, relative, etc.). This is so they can interact with you as your friend might interact.

2. After the first person has practiced leading the other across the line, the listener provides verbal feedback on what worked well, and areas for improvement. Use the checklist on page 77 in your Participant's Guide to guide you when giving feedback.

3. Trade places. Repeat steps one and two.

VIDEO VIGNETTE & PRACTICE: CROSSING THE LINE

CROSSING THE LINE CHECKLIST

Check those points of crossing the line which your partner included in his or her presentation. Use the space provided for additional comments.

ITEM	OBSERVATIONS
Assessing Readiness: *(check one of the following)* ❏ Have you come to the point of asking for God's forgiveness and leadership in your life, or are you still in the process of thinking it through? ❏ Where would you say you are right now in that process? ❏ Is there any reason you wouldn't want to receive God's gift of forgiveness and leadership right now?	**What worked well:**
Praying: ❏ Ask for God's forgiveness ❏ Ask for God's leadership ❏ Give thanks	**Areas for Improvement:**

SESSION SUMMARY

In this session you:

- Practiced telling your personal story

- Identified the steps in leading a person "across the line of faith"

- Practiced praying with someone to receive Christ

SUGGESTED READING: CHAPTER 13

(*Becoming a Contagious Christian* companion book)

In order to expand your understanding of this, the culmination point of contagious Christianity, we encourage you to read Chapter 13, "Crossing the Line of Faith." Doing so will help you increase your readiness to personally usher someone into a relationship with Christ.

Putting It Together

In Session 7 you will:

1. Practice the steps of Relational Evangelism (from transitioning to a spiritual conversation through "crossing the line" of faith)

2. Identify tips for telling people about Christ

PARTNER ACTIVITY—*PUTTING IT TOGETHER*

DIRECTIONS

This activity will include:

- Transitioning to a spiritual conversation

- Explaining a Gospel illustration

- Crossing the line, which includes:
  Assessing readiness
  Praying
  Celebrating their commitment
  Taking the next step (if you have time)

1. Partner with someone you feel comfortable with. Select a scenario (found on pages 81–82) that you might find your-self in with the #1 person on your *Impact List*—or use your own scenario. Use the checklist on pages 83–84 as a guideline for this practice.

2. Briefly (30 seconds) tell your partner this person's first name, the nature of your relationship (neighbor, co-worker, relative, etc.), and the scenario you will be using. This will help your partner interact with you as the person on your *Impact List* might interact. (Remember, for this activity, the *Impact List* person is ready to receive Christ.) Suggestion: Begin the practice by stating the transition statement.

3. After the first person has presented, the listener provides verbal feedback on what worked well and what areas could be improved. Use the checklist on pages 83–84 to guide you when giving feedback.

4. Then trade places. Repeat steps two and three.

PARTNER ACTIVITY: PUTTING IT TOGETHER

Scenario #1:

Your friend (or relative) attends Alcoholics Anonymous (or another support group). Earlier, you had a number of discussions about the difference between believing in a generic "higher power" and trusting in Jesus Christ. You gave them information (a book, tape, etc.) explaining the evidence which supports Christ's claims that He is God and the way to salvation.

You've just finished playing tennis/basketball, etc. You ask about the information you gave them. They reply: "Well, I've been reading the book (listening to the tape) you gave me. I've got to admit it's helping me understand why you believe what you do."

Sample Transition Statement (to a Gospel illustration): "I'm glad to hear that. You know, it's occurred to me that we've talked a lot about God, but not so much about how we can come to know Him personally. . . . If it would be okay, there's an illustration I'd like to share with you that really helped me on this. . ."

Or, if you'd like to use your own transition, write it here:

_____

_____

(Now go to page 83 to select the Gospel illustration to present.)

Scenario #2:

You are talking with your *Impact List* person about a funeral that both of you attended. It was for a co-worker (or mutual acquaintance) who was killed in a car accident.

Sample Transition Statement (to a Gospel illustration): "You know, we've talked before about how important it is to know that if you died you'd be ready. If it's all right, I'd like to explain something to you that tells how we can know we'll go to heaven."

Or, if you'd like to use your own transition, write it here:

_____

_____

(Now go to page 83 to select the Gospel illustration to present.)

PARTNER ACTIVITY: PUTTING IT TOGETHER

Scenario #3:

Your friend/relative is experiencing a lot of problems in their life. You two have already discussed how she/he needs God's help. Now they begin to complain once again about the problems they are experiencing.

Sample Transition Statement (to a Gospel illustration): "I'm really sorry that you have to go through that. You know, we've talked before about how God can help you in these areas . . . The big question is, how do you get into that kind of a relationship with God? Would it be okay if I pass on something that helps to answer that question?"

Or, if you'd like to use your own transition, write it here:

_____

_____

(Now go to page 83 to select the Gospel illustration to present.)

Scenario #4:

The last time you two were together, you had given her/him a book which answered frequently-asked questions about Christianity. This is the first time you have gotten together since then. You have been discussing a variety of topics, such as work/the kids/home improvement projects, etc.

Sample Transition Statement (to a Gospel illustration): "By the way, I hope that book I gave you has helped answer some of your questions about God. . . . You know, I recently heard an illustration that I thought might help clarify the big picture of what Christianity is all about. Are you interested?

Or, if you'd like to use your own transition, write it here:

_____

_____

(Now go to page 83 to select the Gospel illustration to present.)

PARTNER ACTIVITY: PUTTING IT TOGETHER

"PUTTING IT TOGETHER" CHECKLIST

Impact List Person (first name): _____

Use a transition statement:

❏ Use the sample or the one you wrote on pages 81–82.

Present a Gospel illustration:

❏ Do vs. Done

❏ The Bridge

❏ Other: _____

Crossing the line:

1. **Assess readiness** *(three questions you can use)*:

   ❏ Have you come to the point of trusting Christ, or are you still in the process of thinking it through?

   ❏ Where would you say you are right now in that process?

   ❏ Is there any reason you wouldn't want to ask God for His forgiveness and leadership right now?

PARTNER ACTIVITY: PUTTING IT TOGETHER

Checklist, cont.

2. Pray *(three areas in which to prompt them)*:

❐ Ask for God's forgiveness

❐ Ask for God's leadership

❐ Give God thanks

3. Celebrate their commitment:

❐ Acknowledge what has just happened

4. Take the next step *(as time allows)*:

❐ Get involved with other Christians   ❐ Pray

❐ Read the Bible   ❐ Relate to non-believers

Feedback Section

What Worked Well?	Areas for Improvement

TIPS FOR TELLING PEOPLE ABOUT CHRIST

DON'T GIVE A SPEECH

* Principle of "Putting Others First"

GIVE IT IN _____

TALK TO PEOPLE _____

BE _____

ADVICE FOR NEW BELIEVERS:

* Be careful of overzealousness

* Be yourself—don't mimic the style of the person who reached you

* Never underestimate what God can do through you *now*

SESSION SUMMARY

In this session you:

- Practiced the steps of Relational Evangelism (from transitioning to a spiritual conversation to "crossing the line" of faith)

- Identified tips for telling people about Christ

SUGGESTED READING: CHAPTERS 14–15

(*Becoming a Contagious Christian* companion book)

To expand on the exciting implications of what you just practiced, read the final two chapters of *Becoming a Contagious Christian*. Chapter 14 is called "Contagious Christians and Contagious Churches." It will help you envision what it can be like to have a whole church partnering with its members to become more contagious. Chapter 15 challenges all of us to focus our energies where they can make the greatest difference. It's called "Investing Your Life in People."

Objection!

In Session 8 you will:

1. Identify common objections

2. Practice responding to objections

3. List points to remember for our approach
   and attitude

VIDEO VIGNETTE: ANSWERING OBJECTIONS, PART 1

The questions raised in the video are listed below. A paraphrased answer for each question is provided on pages 90–99, which you will be given time to read later.

1. Don't all the religions basically teach the same things, but just use different names for God?

2. As long as each person is genuinely sincere, what difference does it make what they believe?

3. Isn't it narrow-minded for Christians to think that they're right and everyone else is wrong?

4. What credentials back up the claims of Christianity? Is there any good evidence to support it?

5. What makes you so confident that the Bible is true? It has so many authors, so many translations, and was written over so many years—there *must* be mistakes!

INDIVIDUAL EXERCISE: ANSWERING OBJECTIONS, PART 1

If you will turn to page 90 in your Participant's Guide, you will see the first objection Joanne addressed. The information in italics is the paraphrased answer given on the video. Then you will see other information—not in italics—that also can be used to answer the question.

1. Select the one objection out of the five listed that is most likely to come up in a conversation, perhaps a conversation with the first person on your *Impact List*.

2. Read through the information under that objection. Use those parts that you feel comfortable saying to form your own response.

3. Outline your answer using the shaded space to the right of the information. You will use it in a few minutes to practice from.

INDIVIDUAL EXERCISE: ANSWERING OBJECTIONS, PART 1

On the following pages are the questions and objections raised in Part 1 of the video vignette. The answers given in the video are paraphrased and shown in *italics*. Additional responses to each question are also provided.

Video Vignette—Part 1	Outline
1. Don't all the religions basically teach the same things, but just use different names for God? • *When you look beneath the surface, you'll find out that there are major differences between the religions—even including contradictions about who God is. For example, some forms of Buddhism don't even teach that there is a God; Hinduism teaches that God exists and that everything is part of Him; Christianity teaches that God exists, but that He is separate from all He has created. These are mutually exclusive definitions that can not possibly be descriptive of the same God.* • Other religions generally view Jesus as being on more or less the same level as other prophets from God, not as who He claimed to be: the unique incarnation of God who came to earth as a man (John 1:1,14; John 8:24; Phil. 2:5–11). • Other religions deny the biblical teaching that Jesus' ultimate mission was to give His life on the cross as a payment for our sins (Matthew 20:28). They also overlook the fact that of all the religions in history with leaders claiming to be prophets from God, Jesus alone backed up His claims by rising from the dead.	

INDIVIDUAL EXERCISE: ANSWERING OBJECTIONS, PART 1

Objections, continued

Video Vignette—Part 1	Outline
• In both Old Testament and New Testament days there were other religions in existence, and these were clearly *not* viewed by the biblical writers as acceptable alternatives (Numbers 25:3–5; 1 Kings 18:16–40; and 1 Cor. 10:20). For further information about various religions and sects, see *The Kingdom of the Cults,* by Walter Martin; *Cults, World Religions, and the Occult*, by Kenneth Boa; and *Dissonant Voices,* by Harold Netland.	
2. As long as each person is genuinely sincere, what difference does it make what they believe? • *The problem is that sincerely believing something doesn't make it true. You can be sincere, but sincerely wrong. This was illustrated on the video by pointing out that people who get on an airplane that later crashes may be sincere in their belief that they will be safe, but their sincerity doesn't change what is actually going to happen. Our beliefs— no matter how deeply held—have no effect on reality.* • This is true in all areas of life. Sincerely believing it is safe to cross the road doesn't help you if there's traffic coming. Thinking the speed limit is 65 when it's 45 won't prevent you from getting a ticket for speeding. And strongly holding to your beliefs about God doesn't make them true.	

INDIVIDUAL EXERCISE: ANSWERING OBJECTIONS, PART 1

Objections, continued

Video Vignette—Part 1	Outline
• Sincerity did not change the facts or the outcome for the people in situations like the mass suicides of the Jim Jones cult in Guyana in the early 1980s or, more recently, the David Koresh cult in Waco, Texas. • What counts is not the *sincerity* of our faith, but the *object* of our faith. We need to ask ourselves, "Is what I'm trusting in really trustworthy?" Then do our homework to find out whether it is or is not. We need to heed the advice given in the Bible in 1 Thessalonians 5:21: "Test everything. Hold on to the good." For further information read Chapter 1, question 4, in *Give Me an Answer*, by Cliffe Knechtle.	
3. Isn't it narrow-minded for Christians to think that they're right and everyone else is wrong? • *It's not narrow-minded if you've looked into it and found that Christianity proves itself trustworthy in ways that other religions and viewpoints do not.* • Wisdom often leads us to follow a certain course of action over the many other options. For example, when our family doctor prescribes a medication to help us get well, it's not narrow-minded to accept their advice, even though we know there are psychic healers and tribal witch-doctors who would urge a different approach. The question is, who has credentials we can trust?	

INDIVIDUAL EXERCISE: ANSWERING OBJECTIONS, PART 1

Objections, continued

Video Vignette—Part 1	Outline
• Remember that the argument is not really with us—it was *Jesus* Himself who said boldly in John 14:6, "I am the way and the truth and the life. No one come to the Father except through me." • When someone condemns our views for being exclusive, that person is, at that very moment, doing the very thing they are condemning by excluding our beliefs. The important question is whether or not we have good reason to accept our position over all of the other options. • Avoid confusing truth and tolerance—they are two very different things. We should hold strongly to what we believe and communicate it clearly, but also support the rights of others to disagree with our viewpoint. For further information read Chapter two in *Reason to Believe*, by R. C. Sproul.	
4. What credentials back up the claims of Christianity? Is there any good evidence to support it? • *There were detailed prophecies written about Jesus hundreds of years before he was born. No ordinary person could fulfill these, but He fulfilled every one of them.* • Examples include Isaiah 53, which predicted almost 800 years prior to the events that the Messiah would be rejected, that He would "carry our sorrows," that He would pay for our	

INDIVIDUAL EXERCISE: ANSWERING OBJECTIONS, PART 1

Objections, continued

Video Vignette—Part 1	Outline
sins (it says in verse 5 that He would be *"pierced* for our transgressions" —this was hundreds of years before crucifixion had been invented as a method of executing criminals), and that he would come back to life (verse 11). Other key passages include Psalm 22, which predicts details of Jesus' crucifixion, including that His hands and His feet would be pierced (verse 16); and Micah 5:2, which announced that He would be born in Bethlehem.	
• *And there's other evidence, like His miracles, which have been documented . . . and His teachings. He not only taught the highest moral standards, He also lived them. And He predicted that He would come back to life after He died on the cross . . . and He did it!*	
• Jesus' actions were so completely consistent with His high moral teachings that when His opponents wanted to accuse Him of wrongdoing, they had to make up things that weren't true. For example, at the "trial" before they crucified Jesus, they relied heavily on false accusations to build their case against Him (Mark 14:56–59). Earlier, He even challenged them by saying, "Can any of you prove me guilty of sin?" (John 8:46). His point was clear—they could not do so, nor has anyone else been able to throughout history. This is in stark contrast to every other person who has ever	

INDIVIDUAL EXERCISE: ANSWERING OBJECTIONS, PART 1

Objections, continued

Video Vignette—Part 1	Outline
walked the planet, including religious leaders. Jesus alone was blameless.	
• Jesus' miracles were done openly and in broad daylight. They were observed by His supporters as well as His detractors. So compelling was the evidence that His opponents never challenged *whether* He had done them, only the appropriateness of *how* He had done them! For example, when He healed a man's withered hand, they criticized Him for doing so on the Sabbath day (Matthew 12:9–14). Their accusation itself proved that He had actually performed the miracle, which was evidence that He was who He claimed to be: the Son of God (John 10:38).	
• Jesus' greatest miracle—the one on which He staked all of His claims—was His resurrection from the dead (John 2:19–22). The historical record shows that He really did rise from the dead. His disciples, who doubted at first, saw and talked with Him on numerous occasions after the resurrection. This alone can account for the way they moved from fearfully hiding in the shadows to boldly testifying in public, even when it meant risking—and eventually *losing*—their lives. It was an appearance of this same risen Christ that turned Saul, the enemy of Christianity, into Paul, the greatest missionary for Christ who ever lived.	

INDIVIDUAL EXERCISE: ANSWERING OBJECTIONS, PART 1

Objections, continued

Video Vignette—Part 1	Outline
Also, Jesus' resurrection is supported by the fact that His body vanished from His carefully guarded tomb. The Jewish and Roman leaders would have quickly squelched the talk of a risen Messiah if they had been able to point to His crucified body and reassure the people that He was still dead. But they couldn't, because He had risen, and there was no body to be found! For further information read *More Than a Carpenter*, by Josh McDowell; *Know Why You Believe*, by Paul Little; and *Reasonable Faith*, by William Lane Craig.	
5. What makes you so confident that the Bible is true? It has so many authors, so many translations, and was written over so many years—there *must* be mistakes! • *In the drama Joanne answers in two ways. First, she offers a book that will answer Kris's questions about the Bible.* • The first part of this response illustrates what we can do if we don't have a succinct answer at our fingertips or when it doesn't seem like an ideal time and place to go into it. It's okay to defer to reliable sources of information, such as a credible book or teacher or, if it seems preferable, to tell them that we would like to study the question and talk with them more about it in a few days. Our friend is more concerned about getting a *good* answer than an *instant* one.	

INDIVIDUAL EXERCISE: ANSWERING OBJECTIONS, PART 1

Objections, continued

Video Vignette—Part 1	Outline
• *Second, she encourages her to read the Bible for herself to see if God might speak to her through it.* • The second part of Joanne's response was important. One of the most effective ways to help someone see that the Bible really is God's word is to get them to read it for themselves. It will help them get rid of their stereotypes concerning its contents, show them how relevant its teachings are, provide an environment in which the Holy Spirit can powerfully work to convict them of their need, and point them toward the truth. Generally, it is a good idea to direct them to the New Testament as a place to start reading. • If there really is a God like the one the Bible describes, then it would be no problem for Him to guide many different writers in different lands and different times to faithfully record His message. That, in fact, is what the Bible claims He did (2 Peter 1:20–21). An examination of the Bible itself bears this out. The consistency of the message from Genesis through the book of Revelation is astonishing. Most of what people call "contradictions" are easily explained with a little study and reflection. Further, the fact that there are superficial differences in the way the biblical eyewitnesses described what they saw is just further evidence that their testimonies are trustworthy. In other	

97

INDIVIDUAL EXERCISE: ANSWERING OBJECTIONS, PART 1

Objections, continued

Video Vignette—Part 1	Outline
words, they made no effort to "get their stories straight"—they just told what had happened as they saw it. Also, a comparison of the "different translations" will show that they generally just use different words to say the same things. • Jesus Himself endorsed the Bible as the "Word of God" (Matthew 15:6). Repeatedly, He appealed to its authority by saying, "it is written." In the Sermon on the Mount He said that "until heaven and earth disappear, not the smallest letter, not the least stroke of a pen, will by any means disappear from the Law until everything is accomplished" (Matthew 5:18). In John 10:35 He said, "Scripture cannot be broken." Since most people say that Jesus was at least a good teacher, we ought to urge them to take seriously what He taught concerning the Bible. • The reliability of the Bible is strongly supported by history, geography, archaeology, and science. No other religious book enjoys this kind of broad support. Study in these areas has changed the minds of many skeptics who doubted the validity of Christianity, including Lee Strobel, one of the authors of this course (you can read the details of what convinced him to turn from atheism to Christianity in his book, *Inside the Mind of Unchurched Harry and Mary*).	

INDIVIDUAL EXERCISE: ANSWERING OBJECTIONS, PART 1

Objections, continued

Video Vignette—Part 1	Outline
For further information read the section on "Questions about the Bible" in *When Skeptics Ask*, by Norman Geisler and Ron Brooks. Also, to address alleged contradictions in the Bible see *When Critics Ask*, by Norman Geisler and Thomas Howe, and *Encyclopedia of Bible Difficulties*, by Gleason Archer.	

PARTNER ACTIVITY: RESPONDING TO OBJECTIONS, PART 1

DIRECTIONS

Refer back to the answer you just outlined.

1. Tell your partner which objection you are practicing and have them actually ask you the question.

2. Practice your response while they listen.

3. Then switch roles.

VIDEO VIGNETTE: ANSWERING OBJECTIONS, PART 2

6. How do you know that God exists?

7. If a loving and powerful God really exists, why doesn't He do something about all of the evil in the world?

8. What about innocent people who suffer, like little children? Why doesn't God do something to help them?

INDIVIDUAL EXERCISE: ANSWERING OBJECTIONS, PART 2

On the following pages are the questions and objections raised in Part 2 of the video vignette. The answers given in the video are paraphrased and shown in *italics*. Additional responses to each question are also provided.

Video Vignette—Part 2	Outline
6. How do you know that God exists?	
• *Scientific research points to the order in the universe, and that it is precisely suited for human life. One of many examples of this is that even the slightest variation in the tilt of the earth's axis would result in our either freezing or burning up.*	
• *We see order in the human body. We know that something as complex as a wristwatch had to have been made by an intelligent designer. But the hand that wears the watch is far more complex than the watch is, so it certainly must have been made by an intelligent designer. Think how much more this must be true of the whole human body!*	
• *Written history—both inside and outside the Bible (including Jewish, Roman, Greek, and other sources)—support the miraculous events surrounding the life of Jesus. Examples include His fulfilling prophecies recorded hundreds of years earlier, performing miracles in broad daylight in front of both followers and detractors, and His ultimate miracle, rising from the dead three days after He was brutally put to death on a cross.*	
• *Tom pointed to the hard-to-argue-with fact that God has changed his life. It is a change hard to account for in any other way than by pointing to Him.*	

INDIVIDUAL EXERCISE: ANSWERING OBJECTIONS, PART 2

Objections, continued

Video Vignette—Part 2	Outline
• Other arguments can be given, such as God being the only adequate cause for the existence of the universe (otherwise it was either eternal itself or it produced itself out of nothing), and God being the only adequate source of morality among humans (otherwise nothing is really right or wrong —we are only left with preferences). But most people don't need to be overwhelmed with reasons as much as to know that *you* have thought through this important question and accept God's existence for reasons —not on blind faith. For further information read *Can a Man Live Without God?*, by Ravi Zacharias; *The Creator and the Cosmos*, by Hugh Ross; and *Scaling the Secular City*, by J. P. Moreland.	
7. If a loving and powerful God really exists, why doesn't He do something about all of the evil in the world? • *This is a difficult question that I still struggle with at times. One thing that has helped me with it, though, is the realization that the evil isn't all out there. There is evil in me and in you, too. If God decided to get rid of all of the evil, He'd have to destroy us as well.* • God created us with the ability to love and follow Him or to reject and turn away from Him. We chose to rebel against Him and to follow our own inclinations. Romans 3:23 explains that we "all have sinned and fall short of the	

INDIVIDUAL EXERCISE: ANSWERING OBJECTIONS, PART 2

Objections, continued

Video Vignette—Part 2	Outline
glory of God," and Romans 6:23 adds that "the wages of sin is death . . ." Knowing that we are all part of "the evil" that people say "God should do something about" gives us a new and important perspective.	

- *The Bible does say that God will one day judge all evil. But right now, He is patiently giving us an opportunity to turn to Him and receive the forgiveness and life that He offers.*

- God promises that He will put an end to evil. But He hasn't done so yet. He's waiting, because we matter to Him and He wants more of us to turn to Him. The Bible says in 2 Peter 3:9b, "He is patient with you, not wanting anyone to perish, but everyone to come to repentance." But we must not take His patience for granted—there's no way of knowing how long we'll have to receive His mercy and forgiveness.

- Contrary to what we might first think, the existence of evil should lead us *toward* belief in God, not away from it. If there were no God, then there would be no standard of right and wrong. We would have come into existence by chance, and whatever we do would have no meaning or moral value, positive or negative. Some people claim to believe that to be the case, but it's impossible for them to consistently live out that

INDIVIDUAL EXERCISE: ANSWERING OBJECTIONS, PART 2

Objections, continued

Video Vignette—Part 2	Outline
belief. As soon as they protest that someone has "wronged" them or that something is "unfair," they betray their belief in standards that are ultimately above all of us—standards that come not from ourselves, but from the One who made us. For further information read the section on "Questions about Evil" in *When Skeptics Ask*, by Norman Geisler; and *The Problem of Pain*, by C. S. Lewis.	
8. What about innocent people who suffer, like little children? Why doesn't God do something to help them? • *In the video Tom responded very personally by telling about his son Brian's premature birth. It illustrated the kind of situations we sometimes face that make us choose whether to turn to God or away from Him. Tom doesn't claim to understand all the "whys" of what happened, but affirms that God was there to meet him in his pain.* • Avoid giving simplistic answers to this very difficult question. Many times people raise it out of their own pain more than out of a desire to hear a rational answer. Often their need is for Christian care, not Christian answers. Tom proceeded carefully by using His own experience as a point of identification with Frank.	

INDIVIDUAL EXERCISE: ANSWERING OBJECTIONS, PART 2

Objections, continued

Video Vignette—Part 2	Outline
• *Tom goes on to tell of his realization that God understood what he was going through—His Son had suffered, too, when He came to earth. This, Tom says, helped him open up to and experience God's comfort and support.*	
• To God, the suffering caused by evil is not some abstract idea. Remember that God came to earth as a man for the purpose of taking our evil and its penalty on His back when he died on the cross. In 1 Peter 2:24 it says, "He himself bore our sins in his body on the tree, so that we might die to sins and live for righteousness; by his wounds you have been healed." The truth is, Christ suffered under evil in ways that none of us ever will.	
• *Finally, Tom mentions that the Bible is realistic about the condition of the world we live in.*	
• In an age where so many religions and philosophies are trying to convince us that things are getting better and better, or that evil isn't real, it's heartening to see how realistic the Bible is about the world around us. Just watch the six o'clock news or look at some of the struggles in your own life and you'll see how accurate Jesus was when He said in John 16:33, "In this world you will have trouble. But take heart! I have overcome the world." Suffering certainly is a problem, but we see Christianity's	

INDIVIDUAL EXERCISE: ANSWERING OBJECTIONS, PART 2

Objections, continued

Video Vignette—Part 2	Outline
credibility in that it accurately and honestly portrays that problem. • Point out that most of the evil in the world stems from people hurting other people—something God tells us not to do! He *could* stop us from harming each other, but He'd have to limit or take away our freedom to do it. Needless to say, most people are not interested in having God limit their independence. For His own reasons, God lets us choose which way to go in the hope that many of us will turn from our self-centeredness to follow Him. For further information read Chapter 10 in *Know Why You Believe*, by Paul Little; and *When God Doesn't Make Sense*, by James Dobson.	

PARTNER ACTIVITY: RESPONDING TO OBJECTIONS, PART 2

DIRECTIONS

1. Tell your partner which objection you are practicing and have them actually ask you the question.

2. Practice your response while they listen.

3. Then switch roles.

POINTS TO REMEMBER

Always be prepared to give an answer to everyone who asks you to give the reason for the hope that you have. But do this with gentleness and respect (1 Peter 3:15).

APPROACH

- Questions are legitimate

- Look out for _____

- Address the objection, then return to the Gospel message

- Move from the _____ to the _____

ATTITUDE

- Questions need to be dealt with in a spirit of gentleness

- It is important to show _____

- Maintain _____

SESSION SUMMARY

In this session you:

- Identified common objections

- Practiced responding to objections

- Listed points to remember for our attitude and approach

SUGGESTED READING: CHAPTER 12

(*Becoming a Contagious Christian* companion book)

To explore other kinds of obstacles that we sometimes need to help people overcome before they'll be willing to cross the line of faith, read Chapter 12, "Breaking the Barriers to Belief."

COURSE SUMMARY

LOST PEOPLE MATTER TO GOD

EVANGELISM STYLES

- Confrontational
- Intellectual
- Testimonial
- Interpersonal
- Invitational
- Serving

STARTING SPIRITUAL CONVERSATIONS

- Direct method
- Indirect method
- Invitational method

YOUR STORY—THREE HANDLES

1. BC—Before Christ
2. ✝—Conversion
3. AD—After Christ

HIS STORY—THE FOUR POINTS OF THE GOSPEL MESSAGE

1. God
   - God is loving
   - God is holy (absolutely pure)
   - God is just (a good judge)
2. Us
   - We were created good, but became sinful
   - We deserve death (physical and spiritual)
   - We are spiritually helpless ("morally bankrupt")

COURSE SUMMARY

3. Christ
   - Is God, who also became man
   - Died and rose as our substitute
   - Offers His forgiveness as a gift
4. You
   - Must respond
   - Receive Christ as forgiver and leader
   - Undergo a spiritual transformation by the Holy Spirit

CROSSING THE LINE

1. Assess readiness
   - Have you ever come to the point of asking for God's forgiveness and leadership in your life, or are you still in the process of thinking it through?
   - Where would you say you are right now in the process?
   - Is there any reason you wouldn't want to receive God's gift of forgiveness and leadership right now?
2. Pray
   - Ask for God's forgiveness
   - Ask for God's leadership
   - Give thanks
3. Celebrate commitment
4. Take the next step
   - Get involved with other Christians
   - Pray
   - Read the Bible
   - Relate to non-believers

COURSE EVALUATION

BECOMING A CONTAGIOUS CHRISTIAN MATERIAL

1. To what extent did this program meet your expectations in terms of value and quality?

5	4	3	2	1
Went Beyond Expectations		Met Expectations		Less Than Expected

2. How much learning did you experience during this program?

5	4	3	2	1
Significant		Moderate		Little

3. How relevant is what you learned to your church or ministry?

5	4	3	2	1
Highly Relevant		Somewhat Relevant		Not Relevant

4. Would you recommend that others attend this program?

5	4	3	2	1
Yes Definitely		Possibly		Definitely not

5. What aspects of this program were most useful?

_____

_____

6. What aspects of this program were least useful?

_____

_____

COURSE EVALUATION

7. What, if anything, should have been included that was not?

_____

_____

_____

Instructor

8. To what extent did the instructor demonstrate depth of understanding and credibility with regard to the material?

5	4	3	2	1
To a very great extent		To some extent		To little or no extent

9. To what extent did the instructor have a motivating effect, contributing to your learning?

5	4	3	2	1
To a very great extent		To some extent		To little or no extent

10. To what extent did the instructor's interaction with the participants facilitate your learning?

5	4	3	2	1
To a very great extent		To some extent		To little or no extent

11. Comments:

_____

_____

_____

_____

_____

ILLUSTRATIONS

X'S AND O'S

For the person who thinks that if his or her good deeds outnumber the bad deeds, then everything will be okay.

Imagine two score-cards. The first score-card is for good deeds, with an O for every good deed. The second scorecard is for bad deeds, with an X for every bad deed.

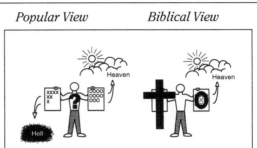

Many people think that as long as they have more O's than X's, they will be all right. So they misbehave on Saturday night and get an X, and then they go to church on Sunday thinking they'll get an O that will offset the X. Their hope is that they'll end up with more O's than X's, and therefore go to heaven.

Regrettably, there are some major problems with this view:

1. First, Romans 3:23b makes it clear that we have all sinned. We all have X's on our boards and fall short of God's standards:

    For all have sinned and fall short of the glory of God . . .

2. While we are doing good deeds to put O's on the scorecard, and maybe even feeling good about it, there is a second problem. The Bible also says that our good deeds, next to God's standards, are not very good at all. We find this in Isaiah 64:6:

    All of us have become like one who is unclean, and all our righteous acts are like filthy rags . . .

We know from these problems that we really cannot put enough O's on the scorecard to offset the X's. We need to have somebody who can wipe the slate clean for us. That is what Christ offers to do. Jesus died on the cross to pay the penalty for our sins. If we accept Him as our leader and forgiver, then He will wipe the slate clean and give us His righteousness.

This is adapted from an illustration told by Bill Hybels, Seeds Tape M8006.

ILLUSTRATIONS

ROMAN ROAD

For people open to looking at the Bible directly and considering its claims for themselves. Some people need to see the Gospel explained in black and white in the Bible, and this is a good way to do that.

The illustration is shown with the verse and dialogue you may have with your friend.

Verse	Dialogue
Romans 3:23 *For all have sinned and fall short of the glory of God...*	The Bible tells us that *all* have fallen short. That certainly includes me. Would you agree that it also includes you?
Romans 6:23 *For the wages of sin is death, but the gift of God is eternal life in Christ Jesus our Lord.*	We both just admitted that we have fallen short. This verse shows we are in a real predicament, because *the wages of sin is death.* In other words, this is what we have earned as a result of falling short. The good news comes out in the second half of the verse. We do not have to suffer death on account of our sins, because *the gift of God is eternal life in Christ Jesus our Lord.* But it is not enough to just know this—we have to act.
Romans 10:13 *Everyone who calls on the name of the Lord will be saved.*	This verse shows that if we are willing to call on the name of the Lord, to accept Jesus as our forgiver and leader, then we will be saved. Are you ready to take this step?

TIP: Mark these verses in a small New Testament and "chain" them together. In the margin next to Romans 3:23, write "Romans 6:23," which will show that the next milestone in the road is Romans 6:23. Next to Romans 6:23, write "Romans 10:13." Keep this New Testament handy in your purse or briefcase.

ILLUSTRATIONS

THE JUDGE

For expanding a person's view of God and what He did for us. He is not only a loving father, but also a just judge; not only a good teacher, but also the one who died in our place. Since the illustrations is verbal, it can be used in person or over the phone. It is a story that hits with emotion as well as truth.

This is a story of a young person convicted of a crime. The judge, being a good judge, could not just let the law-breaker off. The penalty the law demanded was imposed—a fine of $10,000.

The fine was totally beyond the young person's ability to pay. But then the judge did an unusual thing. Taking off his judicial robe, the judge came around in front of the bench and paid the fine.

The judge did this because the criminal was the judge's child. The penalty had to be paid, but the judge paid it.

You would have to agree that it would not make very much sense for the child to refuse to allow the father to pay the penalty and to insist on going to jail.

The point is that God is a good judge as well as a loving father. As a judge, He sees our sin and says, "you have sinned against me, the penalty is death, but I love you and will pay the penalty myself." Then, as a father, He took off His heavenly robe, stepped over to our side of the bench, and paid for our sins by His death on the cross.

Adapted from *More Than a Carpenter*, pages 114–15, by Josh McDowell, © 1997. Used by permission of Tyndale Publishers, Inc. All rights reserved.

ILLUSTRATIONS

A SPIRITUAL EQUATION

> For religious people who think intellectual belief alone makes them a Christian.

John 1:12 says:

Yet to all who received him, to those who believed in his name, he gave the right to become children of God.

Believe + Receive = Become

This verse has three operative words: believe, receive, become. The equation is that if we **believe** the right things about Christ, *and* if we **receive** Him as our forgiver and leader, *then* we **become** true children of God.

Adopted from *How to Give Away Your Faith* by Paul Little. 2nd edition, © 1988 by Marie Little. Used by permission of InterVarsity Press. P.O. Box 1400 Downer's Grove, IL 60515.

BASEBALL

> For those with misplaced confidence in religion, especially if the person is a sports fan. It fits well with the Do vs. Done and the Roman Road illustrations.

Earning our way into God's favor would be like a baseball player trying to get into an imaginary All Universe Player's Association that requires a minimum twenty-year career batting average of 1000, with no errors. God's standard is like that, requiring us to always doing be everything God wants and never stepping outside the boundaries of His commands. Thankfully, that is exactly what Christ, our substitute ("designated hitter"), did for us, followed by dying to pay the full price for our shortcomings.

This illustration is told in detail in Seeds Tape M8914, *Easter Celebration 1989* by Bill Hybels.

ILLUSTRATIONS

NIAGARA FALLS

For those that need a clearer picture of what real faith is. It also shows our helplessness without Christ.

This is about a man who was rolling a wheelbarrow back and forth across the Niagara River on a tightrope. Thousands of people on both banks cheered him on. Next he put a two-hundred pound sack of dirt in the wheelbarrow and rolled it across and back.

"Who believes I can roll a man across?" he asked. Everybody cheered and shouted their agreement. The tightrope walker then asked, "Who will come and sit in the wheelbarrow?"

The crowd grew entirely silent; nobody was willing to risk it. Although they professed belief, nobody was willing to act on it. And so it is with Christ . . .

Adapted from *Peace With God*, by Dr. Billy Graham, © 1953, 1984 by Dr. Billy Graham. Word Inc. All rights reserved. For an updated and expanded version, refer to Seeds Tape M8624 *The Message of the Christian Faith*, part 2 of *Christianity 101* by Bill Hybels.

SWIMMING ACROSS THE OCEAN

For anyone who struggles with self-righteousness, thinking their goodness will somehow get them back to God. This illustration is simple and clear.

Suppose we decided to swim from across the ocean entirely unassisted. You might make it farther than me, and an Olympic Gold Medal swimmer would make it farther than either of us. The fact is that nobody can do it.

That's the way it is with trying to live up to God's standard. We all fall short (Romans 3:23). We all need help from God to make it, and it is Christ who made it possible.

ILLUSTRATIONS

MARRIAGE

For a cultural Christian who "knows all about church and religion," but does not know Christ.

A bachelor may say "Sure, I believe in marriage, I'm sold on it. You should see all the books I've read. I'm an expert on the subject. Besides, I've been to plenty of weddings. Funny thing though, I can't quite understand it. Marriage doesn't seem real to me."

Very simply, this person has not discovered that, to become married, a man first *believes* in a woman, then *receives* her into his life. To get married, one has to make a commitment and say "I do," committing himself to the other person and establishing a relationship. This involves a total commitment.

While we may smile at this bachelor, some of us may be just like him. The parallel is obvious. Someone may "know" all about Jesus, but not know the Lord Himself. Being a Christian requires committing ourselves to a living Lord.

Adopted from *How to Give Away Your Faith* by Paul Little. 2nd edition, © 1988 by Marie Little. Used by permission of InterVarsity Press. P.O. Box 1400 Downer's Grove, IL 60515.

ILLUSTRATIONS

AIRPLANE

For the same person as the Marriage illustration, who needs to understand that, beyond having a right knowledge of the facts, a step of action is required.

We are often like the woman who wanted to fly to another city. She studied all about aviation, discovered which airline had the safest record, went to the airport, found the right flight, checked over the airplane, and even interviewed the pilot, only to stand on the runway and watch the plane takeoff without her.

Many people know all about the Bible, the Gospel of Christ, and the forgiveness and new life available for the asking. But, they never "get on board" by actually asking for and receiving what God has for them.

SCHOOL

For those who compare themselves to others and believe that, because they think they are morally above average, they are okay. This illustration works especially well with students.

Many people assume that God is like their teachers in school who grade on a "curve." However, the Bible tells us that is a false hope. God is completely just and therefore must judge *all* sin, even "average" sin.

The good news is that, while God does not grade on a curve, he will do something even better. He will take the test in our place—and He will get a perfect score! Jesus Christ did that by living a perfect life in our place, then dying to pay the penalty for our sins. Why not ask Him to "apply His perfect score to your grade book" by asking Him to forgive your sins?

WRITE OUT YOUR STORY

_____

_____

_____

_____

_____

_____

_____

_____

_____

_____

_____

_____

_____

_____

_____

_____

_____

_____

_____

_____

_____

KEEPING THE CONVERSATION GOING

After a spiritual conversation has been started it is important to be aware of how the other person is responding. Based on that assessment, determine whether to continue on the spiritual track you are on or shift the topic of conversation back to another subject.

Body language and other signals gauge which direction to take the conversation next. Sometimes you can just test the water with a question or two about spiritual matters. Always be ready to back off, but also be prepared to launch into a full length, in-depth conversation about Christ. The possibilities are exciting!

Listed below are samples of questions that have proved to be quite valuable in keeping the conversation going:

1. What is your religious background?

   What are the positives/negatives of your experience(s)?

   How involved are you now compared to the past? Why?

   What are your thoughts about attending church today?

2. What has been your impression of those people you know and consider to be Christians? Positive or negative?

3. What is your impression of how the media depicts Christianity?

4. What is your perspective about Christian leaders today?

5. What are some of your biggest issues/problems with Christians today?

6. If you had to define a Christian in one or two sentences, what would you say?

7. If you could ask Jesus any question and you knew He would answer, what would you ask?

KEEPING THE CONVERSATION GOING

8. If you had to describe your spiritual journey on a scale from 1 to 10—1 having no interest, 10 being a spiritual giant, and 5 "crossing the line" of faith—what number would you choose for yourself and why?

9. I'd be really curious sometime to hear who you think God is and what He's like.

10. Try these three together (but one at a time):

    What do you think is humanity's basic problem?

    What's your philosophy of life?

    How does your philosophy of life address humanity's basic problem?

Remember, these questions are a tool for you to dig deeper and probe further. These questions help you to draw the person out as to what they believe. Follow-up questions also convey your interest and promote further understanding. They also will help you to develop enough trust so that you earn the right to be heard as to what your opinions are concerning these issues. Use these and other questions like them to develop great discussions!

BIBLIOGRAPHY

Personal Evangelism: to further equip believers

Becoming a Contagious Christian, Bill Hybels and Mark Mittelberg, Zondervan, 1994 (the companion book to this course).

Inside the Mind of Unchurched Harry & Mary, Lee Strobel, Zondervan, 1993.

How To Give Away Your Faith, Paul Little, InterVarsity Press, 1966.

Life-Style Evangelism, Joseph Aldrich, Multnomah, 1981.

Out of the Saltshaker, Rebecca Manley Pippert, InterVarsity, 1979.

Living Proof, Jim Peterson, NavPress, 1989.

Adventures in Personal Evangelism, Bill Hybels, Seeds Tapes Album #AC8717.

Rubbing Shoulders With Irreligious People, Bill Hybels, Seeds Tapes Album #C9023 (includes ideas for building relationships with non-believers).

Resources for Seekers: to give to your unbelieving friends

The Seeker Bible, Zondervan, 1996.

The Reason Why, Robert Laidlaw, Zondervan, 1970 (includes great illustrations of the Gospel).

More Than a Carpenter, Josh McDowell, Tyndale, 1977 (readable presentation of some of the evidence for Christianity).

Basic Christianity. John R.W. Stott, IVP, 1971.

What Jesus Would Say, Lee Strobel, Zondervan, 1994 (a book on modern cultural icons).

Know Why You Believe, Paul Little, InterVarsity Press, 1988.

Give Me An Answer, Cliff Knechtle, InterVarsity Press, 1986.

Reason to Believe, R. C. Sproul, Zondervan, 1982.

Adam Raccoon at Forever Falls, Glen Keane, David C. Cook, 1987 (excellent book for children . . . and their parents!).

Christianity 101, Bill Hybels, Seeds Tapes Album #AM8623 (a presentation of the Gospel message).

Faith Has Its Reasons, Bill Hybels, Seeds Tapes Album #AM8937.

The Case For Christ, Lee Strobel and Bill Hybels, Seeds Album #AM9215 (includes interviews with leading experts).

BIBLIOGRAPHY

Resources for New Believers: to give to your friends who have recently made commitments to Christ

The Quest Study Bible, Zondervan, 1994.

The Seeker Bible, Zondervan, 1995.

Life Application Bible, (Living Bible or New International Version), Tyndale, 1988.

NIV Study Bible (New International Version), Zondervan, 1985.

Too Busy not to Pray, Bill Hybels, InterVarsity Press, 1988.

Honest to God? Bill Hybels, Zondervan, 1990.

Christianity 101, Gilbert Bilezikian, Zondervan, 1993.

What Believers Must Know To Grow, Tom Carter, Evergreen Communications, 1990.

The Compact Guide to the Christian Life, K. C. Hinckley, NavPress, 1989.

Enrolling in the School of Prayer, Bill Hybels, Seeds Tapes Album #AC8536.

Faith's First Steps, Lee Strobel, Seeds Tapes Album #M9009 (a great introduction on spiritual growth).

Seeds Tapes and other materials may be ordered from:

Seeds Resource Center
67 E. Algonquin Road
South Barrington, IL 60010
Phone: 708/765-6222
FAX: 708/765-9222

This resource was created to serve you and to help you in building a local church that prevails! It is just one of many Willow Creek Resources copublished by the Willow Creek Association and Zondervan Publishing House.

Since 1992, the Willow Creek Association (WCA) has been linking like-minded, action-oriented churches with each other and with strategic vision, training, and resources. Now a worldwide network of over five thousand churches from more than eighty denominations, the WCA works to equip Member Churches and others with the tools needed to build prevailing churches. Our desire is to inspire, equip, and encourage Christian leaders to build biblically functioning churches that reach increasing numbers of unchurched people, not just with innovations from Willow Creek Community Church in South Barrington, Illinois, but from any church in the world that has experienced God-given breakthroughs.

Willow Creek Conferences

In the past year, more than 65,000 local church leaders, staff, and volunteers—from WCA Member Churches and others—attended one of our conferences or training events.

Conferences offered on the Willow Creek campus in South Barrington, Illinois, include:

Prevailing Church Conference—Foundational training for staff and volunteers working to build a prevailing local church; offered twice each year.

Prevailing Church Workshops—More than fifty workshops cover seven topic areas that represent key characteristics of a prevailing church; offered twice each year.

Promiseland Conference—Children's ministries; infant through fifth grade.

Prevailing Youth Ministries Conference—Junior and senior high ministries.

Arts Conference—Vision and training for Christian artists using their gifts in the ministries of local churches.

Leadership Summit—Envisioning and equipping Christians with leadership gifts and responsibilities; broadcast live via satellite to sixteen cities.

Contagious Evangelism Conference—Encouragement and training for churches and church leaders who want to be strategic in reaching lost people for Christ.

Small Groups Conference—Exploring how small groups can play a key role in developing authentic Christian community that leads to spiritual transformation.

Prevailing Church Regional Workshops

Each year the WCA team leads seven, two-day training events in cities across the United States. Workshops are offered in topic areas including leadership, next-generation ministries, small groups, arts and worship, evangelism, spiritual gifts, financial stewardship, and spiritual formation. These events make quality training more accessible and affordable to larger groups of staff and volunteers.

Willow Creek Resources

Churches can look to Willow Creek Resources for a trusted channel of ministry tools in areas of leadership, evangelism, spiritual gifts, small groups, drama, contemporary music, financial stewardship, spiritual transformation, and more. For ordering information, call 800-570-9812 or visit www.willowcreek.com.

WCA Membership

Membership in the Willow Creek Association as well as attendance at WCA Conferences is for churches, ministries, and leaders who hold to a historic, orthodox understanding of biblical Christianity. The annual church membership fee of $249 provides discounts for your entire team on all conferences and Willow Creek Resources, networking opportunities with other outreach-oriented churches, a bimonthly newsletter, a subscription to *Defining Moments* monthly audio journal, and more.

WillowNet (www.willowcreek.com)

This internet service provides you with access to hundreds of Willow Creek messages, drama scripts, songs, videos, and multimedia suggestions. The system allows you to sort through these elements and download them for a fee.

Our website also provides detailed information on the Willow Creek Association, Willow Creek Community Church, WCA Membership, conferences, training events, resources, and more.

Willow Creek Association
P.O. Box 3188
Barrington, IL 60011-3188
Phone: 800-570-9812
Fax: 888-922-0035
Web: www.willowcreek.com

Readiness Scale

Level	4 Cynic	3 Skeptic	2 Spectator	1 Seeker	Receives Christ
Characterized by	*Hostility.* Not interested or open to being influenced.	*Disbelief.* May be slightly open, but plagued by doubts.	*Indifference.* May be open to ideas, but not motivated to apply anything personally.	*Interest.* Growing degree of openness; wants to know the truth and follow it.	
Suggested Approach	Ask questions to try to get at the reason for their hostility.	Ask questions to try to diagnose the source of their doubts (misinformation, lack of answers to their questions, underlying "smokescreen" issues).	Try to help them think about matters of ultimate importance: Why they're here, what their purpose in life is, where they stand before God.	Ask questions designed to identify the barriers that are keeping them from trusting Christ.	
Sample Question	"You seem pretty negative toward spiritual matters, has something happened to make you feel angry toward God/Christians?"	"You clearly have doubts about the Christian message. Can we talk about some of your questions?"	"It's so easy to get caught up in the daily grind without ever asking what it all means. Do you ever think about where God fits into your life?"	"What would you say are the main issues keeping you from committing your life to Christ?"	
Your Response	Listen carefully, empathize where possible; try to help them rethink their response to whatever happened.	Listen carefully, try to answer their quesitons, help them start actively looking into the evidence for Christianity.	Encourage them to not wait for tough times or tragedy to think about these matters. Illustrate from your own experience that following Christ makes sense *now*, as well as for eternity.	Correct misinformation, try to answer any lingering questions, show them that the benefits of following Christ far outweigh any costs, move them toward crossing the line of faith.	
Notes	• *This scale refers to openness to **influence**,* not to discussion or relationship.	• *A person may be very religious, but still be a cynic, skeptic, etc., in how they view or respond to Christ and the Gospel message.*		• *People do not necessarily progress through each of these areas; they can move from any one of them to any other, including directly to receiving Christ.*	